JR. GRAPHIC ANCIENT CIVILIZATIONS

EVERYDAY LIFE IN ANCIENT GREECE

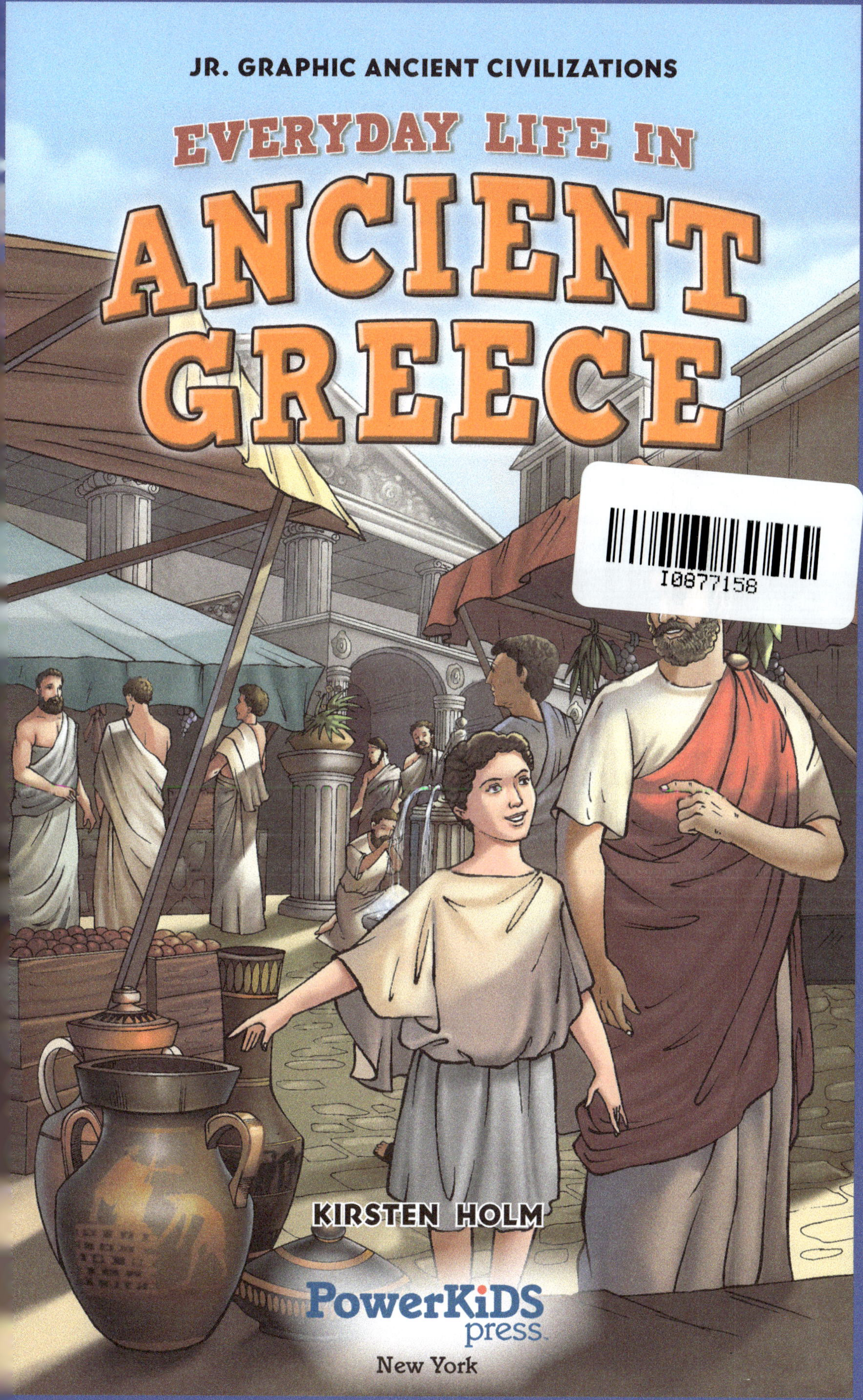

KIRSTEN HOLM

PowerKiDS press.
New York

Published in 2012 by The Rosen Publishing Group, Inc.

29 East 21st Street, New York, NY 10010

First Edition

Editor: Joanne Randolph

Book Design: Planman Technologies

Illustrations: Planman Technologies

Library of Congress Cataloging-in-Publication Data

Holm, Kirsten C. (Kirsten Campbell)

Everyday life in ancient Greece / by Kirsten Campbell Holm.

p. cm. — (Jr. graphic ancient civilizations)

Includes index.

ISBN 978-1-4488-6214-6 (library binding) — ISBN 978-1-4488-6387-7 (pbk.) — ISBN 978-1-4488-6388-4 (6-pack)

1. Greece—Civilization—To 146 B.C.—Juvenile literature. I. Title.

DF77.H646 2012

938—dc23

2011030143

Manufactured in the United States of America

CPSIA Compliance Information: Batch #PLW2102PK: For Further Information contact Rosen Publishing, New York, New York at 1-800-237-9932.

Contents

Historical Background

Ancient Greece was not one country but a group of individual cities that acted as separate countries. These city-states were found mostly around the Aegean Sea. The people of Sparta, Corinth, Athens, and other Greek cities were very different. Spartans were a fierce, warlike people. Corinthians were hardworking merchants and businessmen. Athenians were proud of their strong **democracy**, or *demokratia*, which means "power by the people." Sometimes these city-states fought together against common enemies. Sometimes they fought each other. There was a great **rivalry** between Sparta and Athens.

Athens was founded around 1600 to 1200 BC by Greek-speaking people, although there is evidence that people lived there earlier. The city became increasingly powerful and important beginning in the 800s BC, which is called the Archaic Age. Democracy as a form of government began in the 500s BC with the *ekklesia*, or **assembly**. After Athens beat the Persian navy in 479 BC, it became the cultural center of ancient Greece. During the Classical Age, great playwrights, historians, and philosophers added to Athens's reputation as the center of business and trade.

Sparta **resented** Athens, though. Sparta organized other city-states to rise up and defeat Athens in the Peloponnesian War, which started in 431 BC. After a short time of being ruled by Sparta, Athenians fought back. However, King Philip II of Macedon, father of Alexander the Great, took over the city again in 338 BC. Athens became part of Alexander's empire, which stretched halfway across Asia. This is called the Hellenistic Age. Great philosophers such as Plato and Aristotle lived in Athens at this time. Greek sculpture of this era is still prized today for its beauty.

EVERYDAY LIFE IN
ANCIENT GREECE

THE DAY STARTED EARLY FOR THE SLAVES IN A GREEK HOUSEHOLD. THEY BEGAN PREPARING FOR THE DAY BEFORE THE FAMILY THEY SERVED WOKE UP.

GREEK WOMEN WORE LOOSE GOWNS CALLED *CHITONS*. THE CHITON WAS A LARGE RECTANGLE OF CLOTH THAT WAS GATHERED AT THE WAIST WITH A BELT.

MANY GREEK FAMILIES HAD ONE OR TWO SLAVES. WEALTHY FAMILIES OFTEN HAD SEVERAL.
HYPATIA, COME AND EAT. THERE ARE FRESH FIGS.
MY FAVORITE!
AH, HERE YOU ARE, SILAS.
MEN WORE CHITONS AS WELL, ALTHOUGH THEIRS WERE SHORTER. CHILDREN WORE CLOTHES SIMILAR TO THOSE OF THEIR PARENTS.
APOLLODOROS, IT IS TIME TO GET UP. THERE ARE MANY THINGS TO DO TODAY.
YES, FATHER.

GREEKS ATE A SMALL MEAL OF BREAD, WINE, AND SOME FRUIT IN THE MORNING. MEN AND WOMEN DID NOT EAT TOGETHER, THOUGH.
I WILL SPEND THE MORNING CHECKING OUR FOOD SUPPLIES AND DECIDING WHAT TO ORDER.
PLEASE ORDER MORE FIGS!
DAUGHTERS LIVED WITH THEIR MOTHERS BUT DID NOT SEE THEIR FATHERS OFTEN.
I AM LOOKING FORWARD TO MATH CLASS THIS MORNING. THE TEACHER SAYS I AM FIRST IN MY CLASS!
THAT IS WONDERFUL!
AFTER SCHOOL WE WILL MAKE A SPECIAL TRIP TO VISIT MY FRIEND AGNES, WHO JUST HAD A BABY. WE MUST FINISH THE WEAVING FIRST, THOUGH.
THERE IS *ALWAYS* WEAVING TO BE DONE.

FATHERS AND SONS LIVED IN ROOMS AT THE FRONT OF THE HOUSE.

WEALTHY BOYS IN ATHENS ATTENDED SCHOOL FOR 10 OR MORE YEARS. POORER BOYS WENT FOR ONLY A FEW YEARS.
WHEN I TURN 18, I WILL JOIN THE ARMY.
I WANT TO WORK IN THE GOVERNMENT LIKE MY FATHER. I MIGHT GO TO ALEXANDRIA TO STUDY.
BOYS STUDIED SPORTS, MUSIC, WRITING, AND GRAMMAR.
LEARNING TO SING AND PLAY WELL WILL HELP YOU WITH MATHEMATICS.
STUDENTS PRACTICED WRITING ON PAPYRUS.
I AM BETTER AT GRAMMAR THAN YOU.
BUT YOUR HANDWRITING IS TERRIBLE.

MATHEMATICS AND GEOMETRY WERE TAUGHT AS WELL.
THIS GEOMETRY PROBLEM IS TOUGH.
YOU WILL STUDY EVEN MORE MATHEMATICS IN ALEXANDRIA.
BOYS PRACTICED PUBLIC SPEAKING AND RHETORIC, OR HOW TO MAKE A GOOD ARGUMENT.
I HOPE THAT WE WILL BE CHOSEN TO RECITE FROM HOMER'S *ODYSSEY* AT THE NEXT PUBLIC FESTIVAL.
MY FAVORITE PART IS IN THE CAVE OF THE CYCLOPS!
SEE YOU TOMORROW!

WEALTHY ATHENIAN GIRLS WERE EDUCATED IN MANY OF THE SAME SUBJECTS AS BOYS. POORER GIRLS LEARNED TO TAKE CARE OF A HOME FROM THEIR MOTHERS.
I LIKE MATHEMATICS.
YES, ME TOO. GRAMMAR IS HARDER.
PLAYING MUSIC, SINGING, AND DANCING WERE IMPORTANT SKILLS. STUDENTS LEARNED TO PLAY A STRINGED INSTRUMENT CALLED THE *LYRA*.
I HOPE MY FATHER WILL BE PLEASED WITH HOW WELL I PLAY NOW.
RELIGIOUS FESTIVALS WERE ONE OF THE FEW TIMES GIRLS AND WOMEN PARTICIPATED IN PUBLIC LIFE.
THE FESTIVAL FOR ATHENA WILL HAPPEN SOON.
WHAT AN HONOR IF WE ARE CHOSEN TO LEAD THE PROCESSION!

WOMEN WERE RESPONSIBLE FOR RUNNING THE HOME. THEY MADE SURE THE FAMILY HAD ENOUGH FOOD AND DECIDED WHAT THEY WOULD EAT. WEALTHY WOMEN HAD SLAVES TO BUY THE FOOD AT THE MARKET AND PREPARE MEALS.
EUPHEMIA, FOR THE MEN'S DINNER TONIGHT PREPARE CHICKEN, FISH, AND LAMB. PLEASE MAKE YOUR HONEY PASTRIES, TOO.
WOMEN TOOK CARE OF THOSE IN THE HOUSE WHO WERE SICK. VERY ILL PEOPLE MIGHT SEE A DOCTOR IF THEY COULD PAY.
YOU HAVE CUT YOURSELF BADLY, CHLOE. THIS **SALVE** SHOULD HELP YOU HEAL, THOUGH.
THANK YOU.
WOMEN WORKED ALMOST EVERY DAY ON WEAVING. THEY WOVE ALL THE CLOTH THEIR FAMILY NEEDED.
THIS FABRIC WILL BE FOR NEW CLOTHES TO WEAR TO ATHENA'S FESTIVAL.

WEALTHY WOMEN DID NOT LEAVE THEIR HOMES OFTEN. THEY COULD VISIT FRIENDS ON SPECIAL OCCASIONS AND PARTICIPATE IN RELIGIOUS **CEREMONIES,** THOUGH.

GREEK FAMILIES WERE NOT LARGE, SO IT WAS IMPORTANT TO HAVE A SON WHO WOULD **INHERIT** FAMILY PROPERTY AND WEALTH.

THE GREEKS BELIEVED IN MANY GODS AND GODDESSES. SOME HAD LARGE TEMPLES, LIKE THE PARTHENON. SOME HAD SMALL TEMPLES BY THE SIDE OF THE ROAD.
O EILEITHYIA, GODDESS OF CHILDBIRTH, THANK YOU FOR KEEPING AGNES AND HER SON SAFE.
AN ATHENIAN GIRL MARRIED AT THE AGE OF 14 OR 15. HER HUSBAND WAS OFTEN TWICE HER AGE.
HYPATIA, IN FOUR OR FIVE YEARS YOU WILL GIVE ALL YOUR TOYS TO THE GODS AND MARRY THE MAN YOUR FATHER CHOOSES.
YOU WILL NEED TO WEAVE ALL THE CLOTH FOR YOUR OWN FAMILY WHEN YOU ARE MARRIED.
I HOPE I WILL WEAVE AS WELL AS YOU SOMEDAY.

ATHENS WAS A DEMOCRACY. ALL FREE ATHENIAN MEN WERE CITIZENS AND HAD A VOTE IN THE ASSEMBLY, OR *EKKLESIA*. EVERY YEAR 500 CITIZENS WERE PICKED TO SERVE ON THE COUNCIL, CALLED THE *BOULE*.
SO YOU HAVE ALSO BEEN SELECTED THIS YEAR, MY FRIEND?
YES, THIS IS MY SECOND AND LAST TIME SERVING ATHENS IN THE BOULE.
THE BOULE DID MUCH OF THE DAILY WORK OF RUNNING ATHENS. EVERY DAY A DIFFERENT MEMBER SERVED AS PRESIDENT OF THE BOULE.
IT IS GOOD THAT THE BOULE MEETS EVERY DAY SINCE THERE IS SO MUCH WORK TO BE DONE.
THE BOULE WOULD RECEIVE **AMBASSADORS** FROM OTHER COUNTRIES.
WE BRING THESE GIFTS IN FRIENDSHIP TO THE PEOPLE OF ATHENS.

IT OVERSAW THE ATHENIAN NAVY DOCKYARDS AND ORDERED NEW WARSHIPS, CALLED *TRIREMES*, TO BE BUILT.
THIS TRIREME WILL BE THE FASTEST SHIP IN THE ATHENIAN FLEET.

IT HEARD THE **PETITIONS** OF CITIZENS AND COULD ACT AS JUDGE AND JURY IN IMPORTANT CASES OF **CORRUPTION** OR **MISCONDUCT** BY OFFICIALS.
HIPPOKRATES BOUGHT ROPE FOR OUR NEW WARSHIPS FROM THE MAN WHO GAVE HIM FOUR FINE HORSES.

HOWEVER, THE MOST IMPORTANT JOB OF THE BOULE WAS TO PREPARE THE AGENDA FOR THE ASSEMBLY. IT ALSO CARRIED OUT THE ASSEMBLY'S DECISIONS.
THERE WILL BE A MEETING OF THE ASSEMBLY THIS AFTERNOON. SINCE THERE WILL BE A WRITTEN VOTE, WE WILL MEET IN THE **AGORA**.

IN THE DEMOCRACY OF ATHENS, MORE THAN 30,000 MEN WERE CITIZENS. WOMEN, SLAVES, AND FOREIGNERS WERE NOT.

EQUALITY WAS VERY IMPORTANT IN ATHENS. ANY CITIZEN COULD SPEAK AT THE ASSEMBLY. THE ASSEMBLY PASSED LAWS, MADE **TREATIES** WITH OTHER COUNTRIES, HEARD SERIOUS LEGAL CASES, AND PASSED JUDGMENTS ON THE GUILTY.

ATHENIANS WANTED TO KEEP ANY ONE PERSON FROM BECOMING TOO POWERFUL. ONCE A YEAR, ATHENIAN CITIZENS COULD VOTE TO **EXILE** A CITIZEN FROM THEIR CITY FOR 10 YEARS. THIS VOTE WAS CALLED AN *OSTRAKA*.

TO VOTE, A CITIZEN SCRATCHED THE NAME OF THE PERSON HE WANTED **EXPELLED** ON A BROKEN PIECE OF POTTERY.

THE VOTES WERE COUNTED. IF MORE THAN 6,000 VOTES WERE CAST, THE MAN RECEIVING THE MOST VOTES HAD 10 DAYS TO LEAVE THE CITY. IF THERE WERE FEWER THAN 6,000 VOTES, NO ONE WAS EXPELLED.

WITH THEIR WORK DONE FOR THE DAY, ATHENIAN MEN LIKED TO ENJOY THEMSELVES.

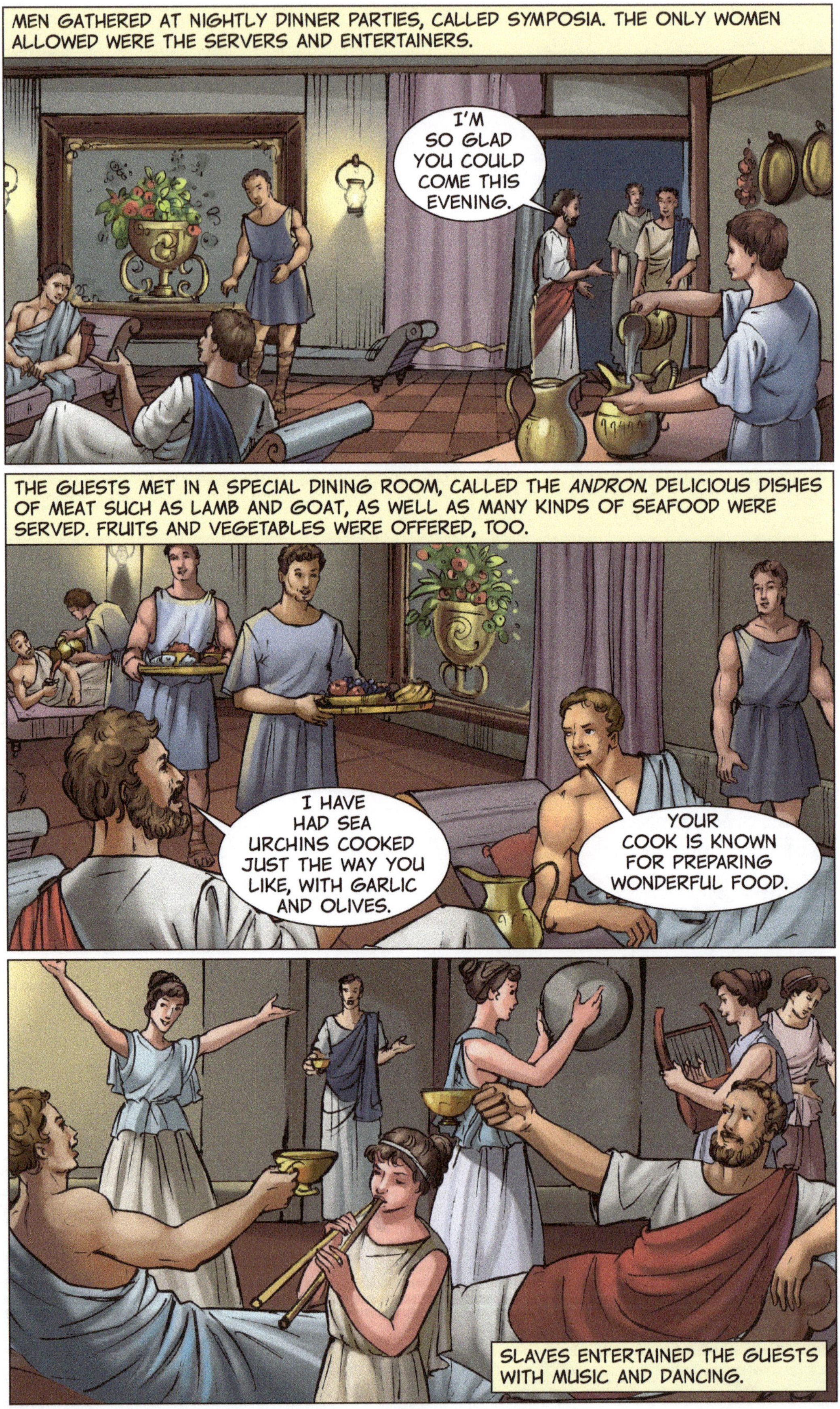
MEN GATHERED AT NIGHTLY DINNER PARTIES, CALLED SYMPOSIA. THE ONLY WOMEN ALLOWED WERE THE SERVERS AND ENTERTAINERS.
I'M SO GLAD YOU COULD COME THIS EVENING.
THE GUESTS MET IN A SPECIAL DINING ROOM, CALLED THE *ANDRON*. DELICIOUS DISHES OF MEAT SUCH AS LAMB AND GOAT, AS WELL AS MANY KINDS OF SEAFOOD WERE SERVED. FRUITS AND VEGETABLES WERE OFFERED, TOO.
I HAVE HAD SEA URCHINS COOKED JUST THE WAY YOU LIKE, WITH GARLIC AND OLIVES.
YOUR COOK IS KNOWN FOR PREPARING WONDERFUL FOOD.
SLAVES ENTERTAINED THE GUESTS WITH MUSIC AND DANCING.

OFTEN THE TALK TURNED TO POLITICS, ART, AND PHILOSOPHY.
ARISTEAS HAD A CLOSE CALL TODAY IN THE ASSEMBLY.
YES. I THINK HE WILL NOT SHOW OFF HIS WEALTH SO OPENLY NOW.
HAVE THE PLAYS BEEN CHOSEN FOR THE NEXT FESTIVAL COMPETITION?
I ENJOYED ARISTOPHANES'S PLAY LAST YEAR. I HOPE HE HAS WRITTEN A NEW ONE.
SYMPOSIA WOULD OFTEN CONTINUE LATE INTO THE EVENING.
GOOD NIGHT!
SEE YOU TOMORROW AT THE RACES!

ALTHOUGH THEY DID NOT SEE EACH OTHER OFTEN DURING THE DAY, A HUSBAND AND WIFE MIGHT SPEND SOME TIME TOGETHER IN THE EVENING, TALKING OVER THE EVENTS OF THEIR SEPARATE DAYS.
THAT WENT WELL. THANK YOU FOR HAVING A GOOD MEAL PREPARED, KALLISTA.
COME, DEMOKRITOS. TELL ME ABOUT YOUR DAY.
HYPATIA HAS BEEN CHOSEN TO HELP LEAD THE FESTIVAL PROCESSION TO ATHENA'S TEMPLE NEXT WEEK.
SHE WILL BE SO PLEASED. SHE HAS BEEN WORKING VERY HARD ON HER DANCING.
THE FUNERAL FOR MY FRIEND PHILA IS TOMORROW. I WILL TAKE SOME EGGS TO LEAVE AT HER GRAVESIDE.
I WILL MAKE SURE THAT SILAS ACCOMPANIES YOU.

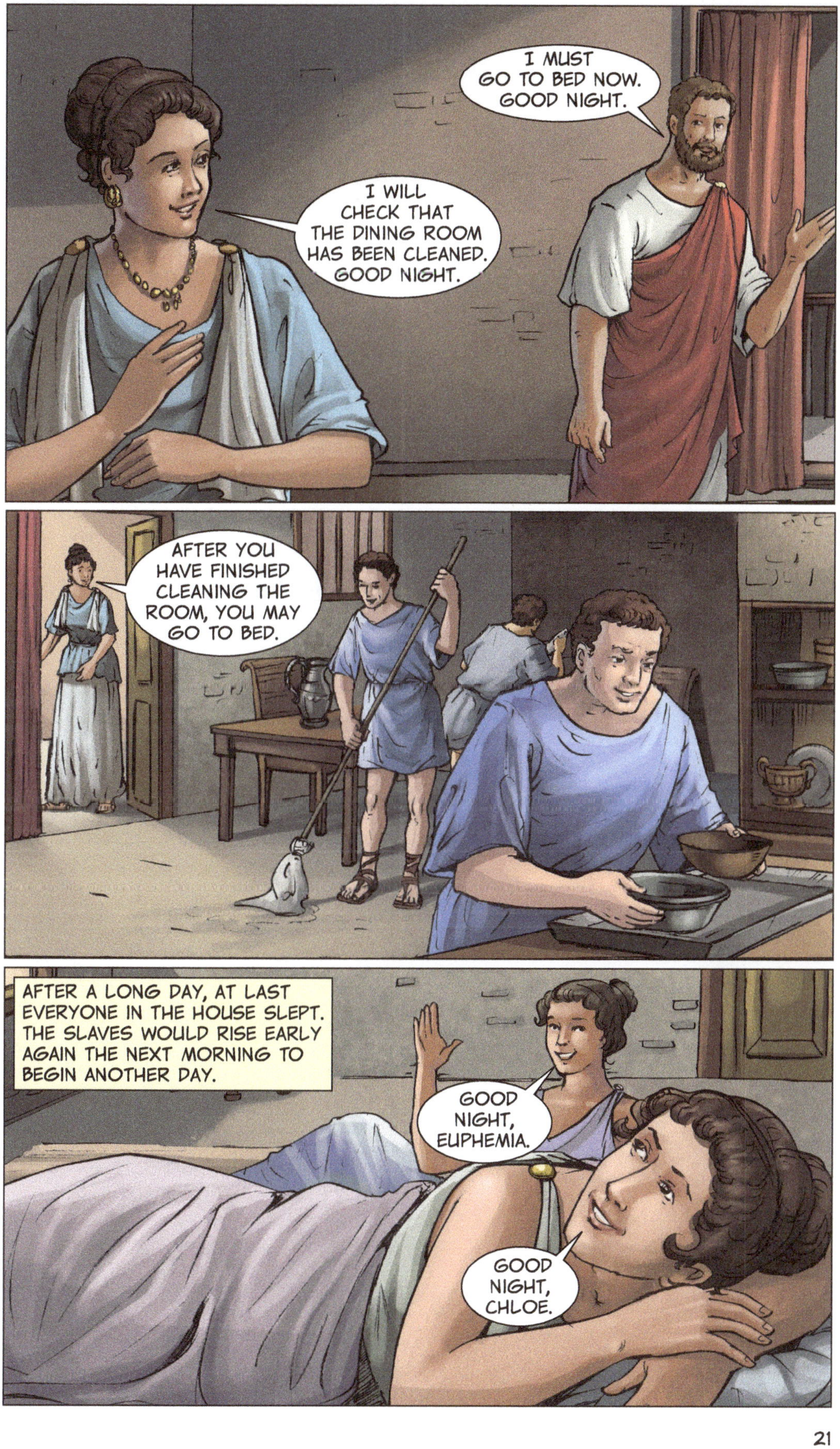
I MUST GO TO BED NOW. GOOD NIGHT.
I WILL CHECK THAT THE DINING ROOM HAS BEEN CLEANED. GOOD NIGHT.
AFTER YOU HAVE FINISHED CLEANING THE ROOM, YOU MAY GO TO BED.
AFTER A LONG DAY, AT LAST EVERYONE IN THE HOUSE SLEPT. THE SLAVES WOULD RISE EARLY AGAIN THE NEXT MORNING TO BEGIN ANOTHER DAY.
GOOD NIGHT, EUPHEMIA.
GOOD NIGHT, CHLOE.

Did You Know?

- Greece was not one country but a collection of cities that were independent states. Athens became one of the most important city-states and ruled over many of the others.
- In the early years of Athens, the rulers were called tyrants. Today that word has a negative meaning, as someone who is cruel to others. At that time, though, it meant someone who used his power to accomplish things.
- The Golden Age of Athens was from 500 to 430 B.C. It was the center for philosophy, learning, and the arts. Athens is often called the cradle of Western civilization.
- In the Athenian Assembly, citizens met about 40 times a year to talk about the issues and vote. Any citizen could talk about any topic in the assembly. Rhetoric, or being able to persuade people, was an important skill because about 30,000 citizens could vote in the assembly.
- Athens's greatest rival was the city-state of Sparta. Spartans were very strict, almost harsh. Boys were taken away from their parents when they were 7 years old and raised in groups to make them tough soldiers. Girls were trained to become strong so they would have healthy children. At 18 to 20 years old, boys and girls took a fitness test. If they did not pass, they were not allowed to be citizens of Sparta.

Glossary

agora (A-guh-ruh) A large market in ancient Greece.

ambassadors (am-BA-suh-durz) Officials who represent their countries.

ambitious (am-BIH-shus) Eager to achieve or acquire things.

assembly (uh-SEM-blee) A group of people who meet to advise a government.

ceremonies (SER-ih-moh-neez) Special series of actions done on certain occasions.

corruption (kuh-RUP-shun) Dishonesty.

democracy (dih-MAH-kruh-see) A government that is run by the people who live under it.

exile (EG-zyl) To make a person leave his or her home or country.

expelled (ek-SPELD) Removed from a place.

inherit (in-HER-it) To receive something after the former owner dies.

misconduct (mis-KON-dukt) Behavior or activity that is illegal or wrong.

petitions (puh-TIH-shunz) Formal ways to ask for things to be done.

resented (rih-ZENT-ed) Disliked or held a grudge against.

rivalry (RY-vul-ree) A match or struggle between two people or things to see which one is the best.

salve (SAV) An oily substance that helps heal a wound.

symposium (sym-POH-zee-um) An evening dinner party of men.

treaties (TREE-teez) Official agreements, signed and agreed upon by each party.

tyrant (TY-rint) A mean ruler.

Index

Web Sites

Due to the changing nature of Internet links, PowerKids Press has developed an online list of Web sites related to the subject of this book. This site is updated regularly. Please use this link to access the list:

www.powerkidslinks.com/civi/greece/